PEACE AND Forgiveness

Jefferson Glassie

Peace and Forgiveness
by Jefferson Glassie

Published by:
Peace Evolutions, LLC
Post Office Box 458-11
Glen Echo, MD 20812-0458

Order books from: orders@peace-evolutions.com
www.peace-evolutions.com

Copyright © 2004 Jefferson C. Glassie
All rights reserved. No part of this book may be reproduced or transmitted in any form or by any means, electronic or mechanical, including photocopying, recording, or by any information storage and retrieval system, without written permission from the author, except for brief quotations for purposes of a book review.

Printed in the United States.

Book Design and Cover Art by Jackie Merritt

Publisher's Cataloging-in-Publication
(Provided by Quality Books, Inc.)

Glassie, Jefferson Caffery.
  Peace and forgiveness / Jefferson Glassie
  p. cm.
  LCCN 2004105570
  ISBN 0-97-53837-0-1

  1. Peace of mind. 2. Peace (Philosophy)
3. Forgiveness. 4. Love. I. Title.

BF637.P3G53 2004   170'.44
                           QBI04-700199

For my children,
Jay, Anne & Max

4

Table of Contents

Introduction 7

Chapter One   *Us* 11

Chapter Two   *Love* 27

Chapter Three *Fear* 43

Chapter Four *Forgiveness* 65

Chapter Five *Peace* 91

Introduction

What is your goal?

Is your goal to have a nice house, a committed relationship, or lots of money? These things will not make you happy, if you are not happy with yourself.

Or do you want something not of this life? Is your goal to reach heaven? How do you know there is a heaven, except based on what someone else told you? Do you know there is anything more than this life on earth? How?

What do you think is? The Universe is what is. The Universe is the life force, the energy, that is everything and that is us. The Universe is at peace. Are you at peace?

I believe that peace is our goal; not just that it should be, but that it is our goal and our destiny. We all can achieve peace, true peace of mind, and peace in our world.

But we are limited by our finite physical forms and the simple fact of our human condition. We are limited by our beliefs and our expectations. Because of these limitations, we have fears. We are afraid that we'll never have the love we want, we're afraid to die, and so we're afraid of the future. These fears cause anger, hate, attack, war, and everything else that is not peace and love.

The way to peace is forgiveness, which simply means letting go. The Universe forgives. You can forgive the past, the future, and yourself, let go of fear, and you will have peace.

Many people do not see what is. They see what others tell them. They believe in myths. They have anger and hate. They do not have peace.

Come with me. Suspend your beliefs. See that you and me and we are all the same. Know you can have peace and that we all can be at peace. Understand that everything from the energy of the Universe is peace, and that the Universe has no fear. Recognize that peace is love, for pure love also has no fear. Learn that anger and hate come from fear and are weak, but that forgiveness defeats fear and is strong.

Peace is yours, if you want it.

Chapter One *Us*

What is? Who are we?

Well, what do you see? I see other people, animals, plants, buildings, mountains, rivers, storms, and blue skies. Some things seem inanimate, yet we know from looking in a microscope and from science that even rocks are made up of particles that have moving components. And it is easy to see and to know that everything else is alive.

You and I are alive. We *know* this. We move, we breathe, *cogito ergo sum*, and all that. We know there is a life force inside us. We've been told it's a soul, but what is that? Soul is really just a term for the energy of the Universe in each of us.

We can see and *know* that dogs and cats are alive; that horses and insects and birds and worms have the life force, too. When they die, they are not alive any more, just like us.

We know plants are alive. They move, grow taller, sprout new leaves and flowers. When you cut open a tree, you can practically see the life inside, the sap and the undulating rings. The life force is with them, too.

Do not the wind and the rain and the snow also seem alive? They certainly have an energy. Something creates the weather. The waves on the ocean never cease. Is there a different life force, a different energy that moves the seas and brings thunderstorms? Doesn't it seem that the force inside everything is the same? How could the energy of the Universe ultimately be different in a flash of lightning than in us?

If you and a fish both have the same life force, are we not then simply the same, just in different physical containers? If we and the waves and the wildebeest all have the same energy of the Universe within us, then are we not all connected and the same at the source?

Yes. We *are* ultimately all the same; different shapes and forms of matter, but all creatures of the energy that is everywhere. Everything comes from this great energy of the Universe. This energy is the absolute force of the Universe. It is either god, or perhaps comes from god.

But who, or what, is god? Is god a he, a she, or an it? Is god a being like a human? Or more like an angel, perhaps?

Do some people have one god, and other people have a different god? I don't know about you, but I have seen no other being that I *know* is god.

What I do know, is that there is a pervasive and all powerful energy that is the force of the Universe, our life source. I see it everywhere; in my friends, in all people, in butterflies and mice and the eagles of the sky. It's in plants and over the hills, in a snowstorm and a drought. It sparkles in the sky and seems to rest at night.

The human mind can create other names and features and identities, but why do we not simply say what we see? There is an energy, and it is everywhere and everything; it is us.

The Universe that is, this energy, is the absolute. It is the source of creativity, of life, of matter, and of death. It is the source of all harmony. Some may call this force, this energy, god. But there are so many different faces to and connotations of the word, that it becomes a divisive term. Universe is a more neutral reference to me.

The Universe does not fear, because it has nothing to fear. Nothing can make it go away; nothing can hurt the

Universe; nothing can snuff out the energy. Since our source is this energy, which is everlasting, then nothing can really ever hurt us either.

The Universe is at peace. There is no conflict. Sure, things happen; stars collide or burn out. Planets live and die. Meteors zoom this way and that, and smash into other heavenly bodies. On our earth home, winds howl and trees crash to the ground. Hurricanes wreak havoc and tornados disrupt the land. Rivers carve stone and rains wash the dirt to the streams. The cells of our body consume nutrition and expel waste, and sometimes consume us. Microscopic atoms collide, too, constantly and everywhere.

Still, the Universe is at peace, because all these things happen and the Universe goes on. The Universe does not judge what happens; the energy does not judge. There is no good or evil in the Universe, only what is. A snowstorm is not good; an avalanche is not bad. An aardvark is not good or bad; an oak tree is not evil, and neither is a grizzly bear. Is it evil when a larger gecko eats a small one, or a sin if a female black widow spider devours her mate? Of course not. Only humans judge in terms like good and evil, and the concepts simply have *no* meaning outside of *our* frame of reference. Good and evil do not independently exist, and there is no sin except in our minds.

Let me express it to you this way. When we look at photographs of the earth from satellites, we see a bright blue, vibrant planet. It looks like perfection itself, and it is. Our earth home is a gem among the cosmos that we can observe.

When we look at those photos, we see a peaceful world. We don't see any national or political or cultural boundaries. There are no lines drawn like on two dimensional maps that separate France from Spain, or Mexico from the United States, or Afghanistan from Pakistan. There is only one earth, with land and water.

As we look more closely at these pictures, as we zoom in, we see mountains and rivers and clouds. Closer still, we see lights and cities and highways and buildings and golf courses and baseball fields. We see planes in the air and automobiles traveling along the roads. Closer, we see people walking and talking and farming and going about their work, like ants or bees building a nest. It looks chaotic, and it is, but it also is not, depending on how we view it.

As we look at the world from our lofty photos, we do not see any fear. We do not see anger or hate or defensiveness or entitlement. We do not see jealousy, or blame, or judgment. Those things are *only* in the minds of humans.

The Universe does not judge these things. The Universe does not condemn or attack. The Universe does not become depressed or angry. The Universe forgives, because everything eventually passes, is forgiven, and is released. There is no good or evil. The Universe just is.

The basic state of the Universe, the energy, is peace. Peace is the essence of the Universe. The energy that is god and is us is peace. Pure peace knows no fear, or anger, or jealousy, or pain, or sin. Because we are energy - at our most basic level we are energy - we also are peace. When you take everything else away, we are energy, we are peace, we are the Universe.

Now, then, what is love? Is not love, the pure love we attribute to god or to a mother's love of her child, the same as peace? Unflappable, perpetual, forgiving; the sweetest of the sweet.

When we love, the love comes from the heart, from our core, from our innermost being. We know that the energy of life, the Universe, is our essence. Thus, since love is our essence and peace is our essence, they are surely the same; love is peace.

Everything eternal springs from this love. It doesn't really matter if we call the energy love, or peace, or god, or the Universe. It's all the same thing. Some may quibble with this. They may believe in other stories and myths made up by their forefathers. That's fine. Beliefs are like snowflakes, as are we; different every one. Yet, I know that all things I see are connected by this energy of the Universe. And to me, the energy is peace and love. That is my belief.

So, when we pray, or think, sing, draw, paint, run, or hum, or when we gaze with tenderness at our children or our parents, we bring out love. At those times, we have peace; we are comforted, and we feel love.

We strive for love, we want to love and be loved. We long for peace and comfort. We do pursue life, liberty, and happiness. We ache to not have fear, to be home, forever. We feel a oneness with the Universe, and we don't want to hurt anymore. We want peace, and when we leave this earth, we will go back to peace and to the energy.

Our being, our soul, leaves the physical form. I do not know where it goes; I do not know where I will go when I die. Some people may have had experiences that they believe show them where they go, to a place of bright light, perhaps. That's fine, but I don't know that.

It seems that when I die, or you die, several things could happen. I may simply cease to be. I may be no more. My life force may go away and my body return to dust and I may never be anything ever again.

Or, I may stay the person I am; that is, my soul may stay what it is, a distinct entity, and I may go to another place - a heaven or a hell, or a purgatory, or a large palace with many virgins.

Or, I - my soul, my spirit - may merge back into the energy, into the Universe. The energy that is me may be poured back into the infinite source of life like a bucket of water into the ocean, never separate or distinct again. Washing and mixing together as waves of water and becoming one with everything else, perhaps with a recollection of who I was, or not.

What does it matter? What will be will be, they say. I do not choose to believe what others - supposedly more learned than I - have told me will happen. How do I know they know? As far as I know, they do *not* know. How does anyone really know if there is a heaven or hell, much less teach others about them?

I do not want to - and do not have to - live my life based on rules, and canons, and requirements for life that some other humans developed, because they thought or believed they would get to heaven if they did those things.

The Universe does not have such rules for individual and social behavior. The Universe does not proclaim that going here on a certain day is good, or not doing something else is bad. The Universe does not care what clothes you wear, or what job you do, or what language you speak, or what you think about god.

The Universe has some attributes that seem like laws; scientists call them gravity, force, magnetism, things like that.

These are just the ways things are. But the Universe does not have a law that says you can't eat something on one day, or have to kneel down now, or worship some deity on your knees. The Universe does not say men can only do certain things or that women can't do other things. Only humans make these rules.

I want to live my life based on what I see and what I know. And I have told you what I see. I see a loving and peaceful Universe, and I see the peace and the love in everything there is. Sometimes, it's hard, because I - we - are only humans in these unusual bodies, with hair, and noses, and ears, and sex organs, and we are limited in what we can see and know.

But when I look, when I think about it, I only see the energy at the most basic state of life. I know this energy, and you know it too. It is you as well as me. We are exactly the same. As fish in schools swimming in the ocean look all the same, and dart this way and that, so too are we the same. And we are the same as them. We are the same energy, the energy of god and the Universe, and we are all divine.

Since we are the same, we are not different. Scientists know that we all came from the same source, from the same small family of human animals that somehow sprung up in the evolution of the planet. Since we are all energy at our core, we are all brothers and sisters in life.

Sure, we're all different, too. Like grains of sand. Everyone different, with different fingerprints, hair, teeth, minds, skills, talents. Some of us are better at some things than others. So, we excel at different activities. Some can dunk a basketball, some can grow corn, others make movies, and other make cars.

Some run much faster than others, or jump higher, or sing better, or understand mathematics more readily. But we are still all the same children of the Universe.

So, if we judge and condemn, as opposed to simply discerning our differences, then we really judge and condemn ourselves. We are unique, each one of us, but we are not better or worse, good or bad, than anyone else. We are all special, but if we think we are *more* special than somebody else, then we fail to see who we are and that we are all the same.

And here we are on earth. For how long, we don't know. No matter what anyone says, we don't really know if we go somewhere afterwards. For all we can see, we do not. The odds are that this life is our only opportunity to live.

If you had only one more day to live, wouldn't that day be very special? If a rose blooms, isn't that flower its own perfection? That flower will never be again. It may not be flawless, but the fact that it is, means that it has attained its own perfection. If something only existed for one minute, that one minute would be that thing's perfection, right?

We are each of us only alive for a short time, a finite period. We begin as nothing, our body is infused with life, with the energy, and then we die and are no more. Then, isn't this life our perfection?

Our lives may not seem perfect; in fact, our lives cannot be perfect, for we are human and are imperfect. Things do not go always as we plan. No matter who or where we are, the practicalities of life interfere with our own view of what would be ideal. But, in the truest sense of paradox, although the life we have is imperfect, it is our perfection, because it is all we know we will ever have.

I do not mean to imply that there is not life after death, or heaven, or hell, or reincarnation. I hope there is something more. I'd like to live again, to live forever. But I do not know that I will, so I choose to consider this life my only one, and to consider it my perfection. I don't want to muck it up and waste energy with anger, hate, violence, or war. It is your perfection, too, and we both have the opportunity to live our lives as we wish and to have peace and be happy.

So, we are peace and love and perfection. Why would you want to be - or think you were - anything else?

Chapter Two *Love*

We all recognize the value and truth of love in our society. Love is *the* ultimate emotion, which binds husband and wife and their children. It is the pervasive force that brings us together, often unexpectedly or even without intention.

Love is most deeply seen perhaps in the oneness between a mother and child. But we also sense love well up when we confront grief or stand on a mountain top and look out, or even when we sing a song.

This sort of human love arises from the abiding love of the Universe. It has strange permutations that sometimes expresses itself in fleeting infatuations, sexual desires, or even controlling behavior. After all, it is human love.

Still, this love we feel and experience is essentially the love and peace of the energy of the Universe. It gives rise to all manner of emotions and behavior in our lives. And all these things further the power and creativity of the Universe as we bring them out.

When we love, we're not afraid. When we act with the Universe, we are creative and strong. When we let the energy flow through us and deeply understand that we are peace and love and perfection, then we can achieve whatever we want, because we will only want love. We must realize the limited nature of what we are - forms of matter - but within that we can accomplish wonderful things, miracles of a kind.

If we consider all that flows from the energy of the Universe, we can better understand our destiny of peace; individual peace of mind and peace among our nations. We also may be surprised at how pervasive these things are, and what their absence portends, as well.

Aside from these examples of love in our closest family relationships, what else comes from the peace, energy, and love of the Universe? There is no one complete or right answer, or any correct order for the answer, but I believe all these things come from the love and peace of the Universe:

Happiness
When you are happy, everything seems right. There is a lightness in your step and a smile on your face. You feel as though nothing can do you harm, that it's all good.

Whether it is the happiness from receiving a present, or having your team win the big game, or getting a raise, or even giving a gift, it is fulfilling and positive and uplifting.

Kindness

Being kind evokes a sense of warmth and a certain pride that you have done a good thing. Every act of kindness, from a smile to the cashier or sweeping the walk for your mother, provides a sense of self worth and meaning. The feeling of acting in a kind manner is even more rewarding than receiving the kindness.

Gratitude

A thankfulness for simply being alive, or receiving a gift or a kindness. This is a feeling that we are lucky, but more deeply that we have actually received something that we deserve. When we feel gratitude, we are happy and content for what we have been given.

Tenderness

When we are tender with someone, we help them to be not afraid and to feel secure. We demonstrate kindness toward them in a way that they know we bear them no wrong. Being tender is strong, because it arises from love.

Prayer

You may call it contemplation or meditation or mindfulness. Thinking and focusing the mind on our innermost self engenders a knowledge of our true peaceful nature. Being comfortable with stillness and our thoughts and the present allows us to touch our true self. You don't need to pray to anyone, or you can pray to many others, dead or alive, or to the Universe or the energy or the temple within. Tapping into the silence of our peace in one way or another brings us closer to the Universe, to the energy, or to god.

Sharing

We share what we have with others and, in giving of ourselves, we bring out the peace and love within us. We are saying, we do not need this or that, we are content and will give to another some of what we have. It recognizes that having things ultimately is meaningless, because we can never in the end have anything except peace and love.

Compassion

The feeling that others are deserving of love and a good life is based on an understanding that we are all the same. This may be focused on one or a few people, as in being compassionate for a poor indigent person or a loved one who is ill, or on all people, as in a feeling of brotherhood with all humans, or even more profoundly having compassion for all living things and the environment.

Reverence

The earth is our home, our mother, and we live here only for a short time. Our reverence for the planet and the other living things here shows that we understand that we are all one. When we are careful and respectful of others and this life, we can feel the peace of the Universe.

Politeness

Our manners and our comportment toward others show that we are gracious and appreciative of them and the harmony and peace that we all cherish in our lives. Silly rules aside, genuine politeness honors the life and connection that we all have.

Truth

Living our lives in truth shows that we are not afraid of things as they are, that we recognize and are satisfied with the state of the Universe. We don't need to make things something other than what they are. Truth and honesty flow from and are consistent with the peace and energy of the Universe, which is the ultimate truth.

Creativity

When we are creative, we leave behind the limitations of our bodies and ordained paths and strike out to something better. The Universe is the ultimate creator, and the source of all things. It is a place of all possibilities and we achieve more harmony and success as we allow ourselves the freedom of possibilities. We may think we fail, but being creative is never failing.

Unity

All things in the Universe are united. We are united with all things. When we demonstrate our union, we bring forth the strength of the energy of life. Divided, we are not strong. Divided, we waste our energy in ways that do not promote peace, like war. Unified, we are perfect.

Art

Painting, singing, sculpting, weaving, or playing the guitar, making movies, or designing buildings are activities of the body and mind that provide inlets to and outlets from the soul, from the energy. The results of these efforts are representations of the creative aspects of the Universe, in other words, love. Where there is art, there is love. And doing art helps keep our body infused with the energy. Art is like prayer for the body.

Acceptance

If we accept, we don't fight or condemn what is. We don't divide ourselves from others, but welcome them. We accept the way we are, our pug nose, scarred forehead, or squeaky voice. We accept that we are worthy. We are not afraid of who we are, for we simply are who we are.

Excellence

We accept who - and what - we are, but we know we can be better in our human endeavors. We can be better golfers, or scientists, or politicians, or fathers. We do not let life have its way with us, but strive for perfection, the perfection that eventually we can't avoid. It is not a crime to want to win the game, be the best, or the smartest, or the fastest. That does not make us better than someone else generally, only better in some human defined endeavor. That effort is normal and admirable. Competition to be the best is simply a striving for perfection. We can't get there in our human form, of course; there *will* always be someone bigger, faster, smarter, richer. The Universe defines the ultimate excellence, and our attempts to get there do not hold us back.

Generosity

It's often said that giving is better than receiving. When we receive, we get something we don't really need (other than if we receive love). We don't really need money, or sweaters, or cell phones. When we give, we acknowledge that we don't need anything but love, and the act of giving stirs up the energy within us and sends it out to others. In fact, giving is receiving.

Fitness

We live in these bodies. We can fail to take care of them, and they will fail us and cause us discomfort; worse, we will not be able to enjoy the life we have been given to the fullest. When we move our bodies around, in work or play, and can walk, run, throw, catch, lift, and travel to other places, we honor the form that our energy has entered and feel more connectivity to the Universe. We can walk to the mountains and swim in the sea. Eating healthy foods and not overindulging helps us do the things we want to do and best experience our world. When we are fit, we feel worthy and positive.

Passion

When you do your passion, when you do what you love and what you enjoy more than anything, that also is love based. When the energy flows through you and you are fulfilled in your art or your work, that is love. Art is love; work is love; creating is love. That is why your passions, the things you love to do, are so fulfilling. The more you do your passion, the more love you will have.

All of these - and many more like them - are based in and consistent with the peace and love and the energy of the Universe. I call them "love based" actions and emotions. You have felt these emotions before, hopefully many times. Think of the happiest moments of your life. Perhaps the birth of your first child, or the marriage of your oldest daughter, or the first time your son scored a goal in second grade soccer.

Think of when your high school team won the championship, or even when your professional team won the Super Bowl. Remember the look of surprise and happiness when you gave a special gift to a loved one, or when you complimented someone you work with on a job well done.

These feelings don't always come in big packages. Think of the nice smile the lady behind the counter gave you this morning, or the sincere 'good morning' a stranger offered you in the elevator. How about the thankfulness you felt when someone did you a favor, such as letting you into the line of traffic or holding the door open for you?

Recall the joy you felt when you graduated from college, or played that song perfectly on the piano for the first time. Think of how much you love your mother. Do you remember the feeling when you first loved your spouse or partner?

Feel the fullness of these emotions well up in you, and you know they are love. Your happiness can cause tears of joy to erupt from your soul when the love fills your heart. There is something so positive and uplifting in these love based emotions. And the most profound are not that different from the most mundane.

Of course, emotions don't last. They come and go, but what they are based on is always there, the love and peace of the Universe. Somewhere inside, you know that. You may not feel these wonderful emotions all or even most of the time; few of us do, but don't you believe that you *could* feel the wholeness and fullness and satisfaction of an abiding peace constantly?

If not, why not? Wouldn't anyone want to feel positive and loved and strong all the time? Why can't you have peace every moment?

The truth is that you can. You may have a wide range of emotions, we all do, but your peace of mind only depends on how you look at life, and most importantly whether you forgive. You absolutely can have peace if you want it.

This is not to say there aren't constant problems that arise from living in this complex world. It's not to say there isn't conflict or chaos or disruption or destruction in the Universe. We have those sorts of things occur in our lives, but we also have the ability to recognize and witness them for what they are, momentary perceptions of deviations from the true nature of the peaceful Universe.

The more that we do and experience these types of love based actions, the more we come to understand the peace of the Universe. These are thought of generally as "good" in most societies, though there is no good or bad in the Universe. They may be considered positive, or strong, or beneficial, or life supporting.

And we do have a choice. We make choices every minute of every day about how we want to act and what we want to do. We can choose to act in accordance with love. We decide who and whether to love. The Universe does not choose; there is no choice in the energy and peace and love of the Universe. We have a free will to decide to be positive, beneficial, and life supporting, or not.

As we go through life, we learn about life. We have successes and failures, fulfilling jobs and boring jobs, good friends and people we think are jerks. As we learn more about life through these activities and all of our relationships, we grow to understand that there are ultimately no successes or failures, no mistakes, and nothing really to have any regrets about.

It is important to strive to succeed at what we do, to seek perfection in our human activities, to make all of our lives as happy as possible. The achievements of science and technology help us to know more and to live longer and more comfortably. We must do these things. However, they ultimately all pass and are forgotten.

What's important is to live and learn, and hopefully come to understand the true nature of the Universe so that we can achieve harmony and peace for ourselves and our world. If we choose to live in accordance with love based acts and emotions, we can have that peace.

Chapter Three *Fear*

So, what keeps us from having the peace of the Universe? The answer is always fear.

Fear is the absence of peace. If we had peace, we would have nothing to fear, for we would have the divine love of the Universe and we would know that nothing truly could keep us from peace. When we do not have peace, we fear that we may not ever have peace.

Our fear arises not from the devil. There is no devil. (Have you ever seen the devil, or only things that you thought came from the devil?) Our fear arises simply from the fact that we're human and are limited in our perceptions and understandings by what we can sense through these bodies we inhabit. We have fears based on our beliefs and our expectations. Ultimately, we fear not having the peace and love of the Universe; we are afraid we will never have god's love. We are afraid of being alone.

The most basic fears are exacerbated by our fear of death and the unknown. No matter what we believe or what others tell us to believe about heaven or everlasting life, we are not sure what there is after death, if anything. We are afraid of not being anymore. We are afraid to die. We are afraid of the future.

Everything that is not love based is "fear based," and arises from our fear of not being loved, not achieving peace, and dying. Most do not recognize this, believing that our misfortunes and sadness come from evil or a dark side. The only dark side is fear.

It is easy to understand the love based actions and emotions. We can all see that some things are positive, as we discussed. We know that a child's innocent laughter is lovely. We understand that the joy of a glorious day in the sun is consistent with love and with peace.

We do understand that some things are dastardly and not conducive to peaceful human life. We know that murder, rape, war, and hate are not representative of love.

But it is far more difficult to fathom that all of the actions and emotions that are not love based are fear based, and that it's as simple as that. Certainly, many acts and feelings have some mixture of the two. Once we understand these things, however, we are on the path to peace through forgiveness, by letting go of our fears. Let me explain some fear based actions and emotions.

Anger

When you are afraid that you will lose something or are not treated the way you feel you should or feel unloved, you get angry. You may feel justified in being angry sometimes. There is a perceived righteousness in feeling angry that someone has done something to hurt you or insulted you or offended you. Know this; anger is never justified. You are only angry because you are afraid of something. We may feel anger, because we have human emotions that are often difficult to contain or understand, at first. But all anger eventually melts away, and no one can ever really hurt or offend us.

Say you're angry at some people of another country. You would not be angry at them if you didn't fear them, fear that they could cause you injury or disrupt your peace or deprive you and your family of a peaceful and loving life. Why would you be angry at them if you didn't fear them or what they might do? What would there be to be angry about?

Or, think of when you were recently angry with a loved one. It may be a child who does not obey you or disappoints you with her behavior in school. You are afraid that she will not act the way you prefer and you will not be happy. You fear that *you* will be subject to ridicule or judgment or criticism from your family or friends or others you don't even know. You may be angry at the child because you are afraid she doesn't respect and love you.

If you are angry at the way someone else acts, you only have that anger because you fear something. You may fear most that you are not worthy or good enough and that you have to fight to protect your honor. You would not be angry and fight if you did not fear for your own peace or safety.

Attack

Would anyone ever attack someone else unless they were afraid? If you were not afraid and were at peace, would you attack someone, either verbally or physically? Attack is only meant to injure another person or to make them feel guilty about themselves, their actions, their beliefs, or their feelings.

A person might attack another because he was afraid of being inferior to that other person or because he would not have something he wanted, maybe money, or wealth, or success. A nation might attack another because its people were afraid for their own peace, or that the other nation may steal its food, water, land, or oil. The believers of a religion might attack others because of a fear that their religion and their way of life was not right or that their beliefs would be overcome by others.

You might attack a loved one with words to say that they were stupid, or ugly, or not deserving, or not right. Are not these all judgments intended to make you feel better than them, and to make them feel bad or guilty about not doing or seeing something your way? You might attack another for fear that you could not be happy with them not in your life and you want to punish them for your perception that they do not love you.

You can't think of an attack that is not based on fear. Go ahead, try it. But when you do, always ask yourself, "why?" Why do you or does this person attack? Don't be satisfied with the initial answer, go further. You will always find that it is based on some fear, and usually most obviously a fear of not having love or peace.

Jealousy

This is an easy one. You are jealous of another person because he has something you do not or cannot have; you're afraid you'll never have love. Or you are afraid that a person you love will no longer love you, and instead will love the person you are afraid he will love. Jealousy is clearly based on fear.

Depression

It is a sadness that becomes nearly overwhelming. It is the fear that one will not be loved, or that one is not lovable, or that one will never have peace and love in one's life. If you had peace and *knew* that you were love and perfection, how could you be depressed? If you felt truly loved and worthy, would you be depressed?

There is no intention here to belittle anyone who is depressed, or whose fear and depression have permeated their consciousness to the point that it is overwhelming. *We all have fears.* But know that there is truthfully nothing to fear, ever.

Low self esteem

One would define low self esteem as a feeling where the person does not believe they are as good as other people. Is that not a fear that one is not good enough? If a person knew he or she was divine love, how could that person believe they were not good enough? If a person has low self esteem, they are only perceiving from their human eyes and mind. They are seeing nothing but their limitations and believing them.

Of course, someone is always better at something than every one of us. Another is always a better writer, or basketball player, or chef, or lover, or speaker. If you focus on the glass half empty, you will always be only half full of love and peace, and staring at the empty part of the glass. There is nothing empty in you. You are perfection in the eyes of the Universe because you are one with the Universe.

Hopelessness

This is an acute fear that one will never be happy or have a good home or find peace. It is amazing that it can lead someone to blow up themselves and other innocent people. It is clearly fear that causes this; fear to the point of abandoning all hope for a good or meaningful life; it is a fear so desperate that it overcomes the fear of death.

Guilt

You never do this for me, you don't do that for me, you have offended me. Do you not think these attacks are only to make another feel guilty and fear that they are not good enough or that you will not love them or that they are wrong? You left me, you won't marry me, you hurt me. Are these justified attacks, or meant to instill a feeling of guilt?

You are never alone if you know you are part of the loving energy of the Universe. You don't have to try to make someone feel guilty about anything. And how could someone hurt your immortal soul simply by doing something that they want to do with their life? Do you need someone else's love in order to feel good about yourself, and do you have to make them feel guilty because you feel unloved? Guilt is only a fear that you have not done something well enough or are bad.

A person may have done something that society believes is not good or beneficial or that is harmful. A person may feel badly that he did not do as he should have; it is still fear based, and comes about because of a fear that the person is not good enough.

Disappointment

You may feel sad and dismayed because you are disappointed in the way someone else has acted. Maybe they can't do better, or maybe it's just that they can't do better in your eyes. But aren't they perfect, just like you? How are they different than you? Didn't you ever fail to live up to your own expectations? If you are disappointed in your children because they do not get good grades or you think they are messy or lazy, who is feeling that disappointment?

It is you and only you, and you're feeling that because of *your* fear that they will not be the types of sons or daughters you'd be proud of; in other words, you fear that your children, and therefore you, are not good enough. Another person is not responsible for your happiness and peace of mind. You may feel disappointed, but that is being afraid something you have done or someone else has done is not good.

You never are really justified in feeling disappointed in someone else, since it's really your disappointment. You also might feel disappointed that you didn't get what you felt you deserved, in the way of money, or gifts, or praise. You feel the draw toward happiness in these things, but of course they cannot satisfy, so you feel disappointment because you are afraid you never will be satisfied.

Judgment

When you make a judgment that someone else is not acting morally, or is evil, or has behaved inappropriately, you are judging yourself, because we are all the same. You are afraid that you are not better than them, so you condemn them. You judge them since you fear that they are right, because if they are right, then you are wrong and maybe everything you believe is wrong, too. You judge them because you believe if they are allowed to do as they do, that you will be harmed or will not have peace. You are afraid or you would not judge.

If you at once realized your perfection and your similar imperfection to other human beings, you would not judge. You can discern differences, and must in order for you and society to grow and learn and understand. But if you make value judgments, then you do so only because you fear you are wrong. If you did not think you were better than someone else, then you would not need to judge them; you would understand and accept and love them. Judge not, lest you be judged too.

Blame

Life simply is. The Universe is. The Universe does not blame. You blame someone for *your situation* because otherwise you would be responsible. You feel it is easier to blame something than simply learn to live as you are. You are afraid that you will not be able to have peace because of what someone else has done. Listen; there is never anyone else to blame for your unhappiness or lack of peace.

You may have emotions that make it hard to be happy. Who can decide to change these emotions? Only you. If your wife left you or your daughter's husband left her or a neighbor drove her car into you, what good does it do to blame? What good does it do to blame and to live with the anger, simply because you fear you can't be happy?

Victimization

The Universe is not fair or unfair; there is no fairness or unfairness. If something happens to you, it is just what happened. Do you think there is even one person who ever lived who did not have something happen to them that they could have thought was bad and unfair? I mean, everyone dies, don't they? Does that mean every person who ever lived was a victim, too?

Being a victim means blaming someone else for what has happened to you and being afraid that you can't face it. You are afraid that you will never be happy or can never have peace. But it's all how *you* look at it. Being a victim also means you're afraid to live the way you want because of something that happened in the past. Being a victim - leaving wounds from the past open - is a waste of energy that does not lead to happiness.

Greed

Another easy one to see the fear; you are afraid that you will not have enough to be happy, so you want more. You want more than other people so you can feel that you are better than them. You want things because you are afraid you can't be happy by yourself. We all only need so much to live, yet we compile more money, clothes, and things than we would ever need.

Sure, you need clothes, shelter, and things to do in your life. Being successful in your endeavors (though success is relative) is fine and seeking it is admirable. But having and wanting too much is not sharing and is not loving. We can't take any of it with us, as the saying goes, so why be afraid not to have it or to lose it?

Defensiveness

Other people may make statements about us that could be viewed as attacks. They might say we are dumb or imply that our size or weight or color makes us less than them. We are insulted. Why? So what? How can what anyone thinks or says about you truly hurt you? When we are defensive, we fear that maybe they are right or that we are wrong or that they are better than us. Being insulted just means that you are angry and afraid that someone will be allowed to think or say something about you. If you were strong and without fear, why would you ever feel insulted or defensive?

Lying

Why would anyone lie, if they weren't afraid of the truth? There would be no need to lie, to cover something up, or to try and make people believe something that is not true, if you were fulfilled in love.

Stealing

Same thing; why would anyone steal if they weren't afraid that what they had wasn't enough?

Entitlement

You feel entitled, because you think you're better than others. In other words, you are afraid that if you are not entitled, you are not better or maybe even unworthy. You have to do and act and talk like you are entitled to special status as a human being. Why? To show everyone that you're worthy and lovable. You don't need to do that, of course, if you already know it.

Hate

When you have reached the very depths, when you are so far removed from love and knowledge of your perfection, then you hate. Hate is saying I could never love you, I don't want to have anything to do with you, you are not like me, you are damnable.

The person who hates is a stranger to love. They may think they know love, but they cannot if they hate. They enjoy hating, because it makes them feel special or different or better. If a person hates, they fear what another person can do to them. But, really, they are only afraid to love that person, because then they would have to give up their anger and their judgment.

Control

Anytime you try to control what someone else does, you are doing so because you are afraid that what they will do will not meet with your approval, and ultimately you are afraid they will not love you. We all attempt to exert some amount of control or influence over other people, so that we can achieve what we want. That is different than trying to control what a loved one may want to do.

No one who truly loves will try to control anyone else. And, if a person is comfortable and secure and without fear, why would such person ever want to even try to demonstrate physical or psychological control over someone else?

Parents may think they control their children; they are actually only helping them grow and learn, and do not really even control an infant. Exerting physical control over someone demonstrates even greater fear of not being loved or of being unworthy, such as through rape, abuse, bondage, or slavery. Attempting to control a wife, or husband, or child through guilt is nearly the same, and destined to provide the seeds for resentment, independence, and anger.

Stress

Where do you think all the stress in our modern world comes from? The air, or traffic, or computers? Seems unlikely, huh? Yes, stress also comes from fear; our fear that we won't get certain things done, or that we won't get to do the things we want to do. If your job stresses you out, isn't it because you're afraid you won't get your work done, or won't get it done well? If your hectic family schedule causes stress, it's not because you hate your kids. You just have so much to do, that you're afraid you can't get it all done and will never have time to relax and enjoy yourself.

We all stress out, because we're just so afraid of all the things we have to do, of all the traffic, of not having enough money, etc., etc., etc.

Pain

Physical pain is a function of physiology. It is a real feeling, but is transitory and does not last. Pain in the form of emotional anguish is not real; it is only fear, the fear of not having love or not being lovable or worthy. If someone is said to be in "pain," they are experiencing the effects of this fear. Pain often comes from a loss, such as grief over the death of a loved one. It can also come from the loss of a relationship, even if only for a brief time, where it is more akin to simple sadness.

Feeling this pain or grief over such a loss is the realization of a fear confirmed and the feeling that one may not be able to be happy or whole again. We develop close spiritual connections with our life partners, and boyfriends or girlfriends, and children, at a deep level. When we lose such a relationship, we mourn the loss. If we were in a state of pure love and peace, we would understand the true nature of such separations and we would not feel the pain. But we are human and we feel such grief deeply, but it too will end, like everything else but the Universe.

Terrorism

Attempting to instill fear and disrupt other peoples' lives is a severe demonstration of fear. If a person is so out of touch with love and peace that he thinks the only way to preserve his beliefs or support his values is actually to harm others and spread fear, that person is very afraid and very weak.

He is afraid that other people will not respect him and his world, or will overcome his beliefs and culture, so he attacks violently. Poor young children shoot their classmates because they feel disrespected and terrorists bomb innocent children; all because they fear the denigration of their self and their views.

All of these fear based actions and emotions are weak, not strong. If you lie, and kill, and attack, you may think you're acting in a strong manner and that you are better than someone else because of the things you do. This could not be farther from the truth. The people who try to show their strength in these ways are so very weak and ignorant of love.

But all of these fears are very attractive. Think of how humans crowd theaters to see horror films, read scary novels, thrive on violent video games, and ride on frightening roller coasters. Spouses have affairs and the fear of being caught intensifies the nature of the acts. Bigotry, and hate, and rape, and beating, and controlling others excites and gives a sense of power, and people can become addicted to this kind of power. Of course, it is a short lived power that does not satisfy, because it is human and cannot be maintained.

One would assume that love based actions and emotions should be much more enticing. They are, of course, ultimately. After the intoxicating thrill of fear based actions is gone, the thirst for love remains unquenched, and by contrast the true satisfaction of love becomes apparent. Some think love and peace are weak; love, and kindness, and politeness, and generosity. But they are the most powerful and strong of all.

Fear is by its nature exciting; we are intensely afraid to die. The fear that causes us to run from fire is a pulsating force and it can help keep us safe in a positive way. Fear of storms, or bandits, or wild dogs allows us to build safe and warm shelters for our families. The fear of making a mistake causes us to do better. Fear of failure creates stress, but stokes the fires of diligence and creativity. There is a blend of fear and love in many of the things we do; for example, we do not want to fail, but more importantly, we strive for excellence.

The fear based actions and emotions arise entirely because of our limited human condition. We are finite in these bodies and must die. We are limited by our five physical senses, the daily routine of our lives, and the short term need for food and shelter. If we knew we would have ultimate peace forever, what would we have to fear?

If we could appreciate our perpetual perfection, understand the fullness of our lives just as they are, why would anyone fear something as mundane as that another person may be smarter, or richer, or faster, or stronger? If we understood our universal identical essence in love, why would we cry when our loved ones go their own ways? If we truly knew we were all divine, why we would judge another? Why would we ever judge, or blame, or try to control someone else?

If fear based actions are an inevitable offshoot of our humanity, then the question becomes, how can we eliminate all of these weak human features so that we can have the peace we seek? Complicated only by our emotions, the answer is easy: *let them go!*

Chapter Four *Forgiveness*

This is the key. This is the key to you finding peace, and to peace in our world.

Forgiveness is letting go of fear. What's left is peace.

When we forgive someone, it is not that complicated. We simply let go. The forgiveness of which I speak is not forgiveness of something wrong, bad, or immoral, although that is the connotation many understand. This forgiveness is just releasing something that happened in the past or something that we fear of the future.

We sort of say, "never mind," to what someone has done or to some occurrence or situation. You may think of it as forgiving a perceived wrong against you; but from the standpoint of the forgiven what they have done may not be (and probably is not) wrong; it's just what happened. They likely thought what they did was right.

There is no need for a long and formal process of atonement or confession of sins. We do not need to put conditions on our forgiveness, because that is only controlling and returns us to the realm of fear.

We see that what has been done is in the past; everything done is already in the past and is no longer of consequence. The past is gone, history, kaput. An act in the past is no more and can not hurt us, unless we let it. Why would you want to hold on to the past if it caused you pain?

Many do not forgive, because they believe the unforgiven suffers if they're not forgiven. That is totally wrong. The one who is to be forgiven may suffer from their *own* guilt, or regret, or sadness, or depression, or other fear based emotion; everyone is responsible for their own emotions and actions, and their own fears. But they do not suffer simply because they are not forgiven (unless, of course, they decide to suffer).

Indeed, if it was true that a person would suffer because he was not forgiven, then withholding forgiveness would simply be an attempt to inflict punishment. By what right does one have to punish another? The Universe does not punish. Punishment is human, and is based on the fear that if certain conduct is not punished, it will be repeated and the results will not be good. So, people think that they are punishing the other person by not forgiving them, and often even deriving "pleasure" from it. In reality, by not forgiving, they are punishing themselves.

When you do not forgive, when you do not let go, you are the one who bears the fear and the fear based emotions. You are the one who remains in pain and suffers. The anger, or hate, or jealousy, or victimization *remains with you*. These things arise from fear, and the fear persists if you do not forgive, if you do not let it go.

It is not only forgiving others, but *forgiving yourself* that is often the most important. When you forgive yourself, you let go of the past or your own fears of the future. If you perceive that another harms you and you do not forgive them, then you keep that anger in your heart directed at them, and love is also withheld. That's bad enough.

But if you do not forgive yourself, you retain the feeling that you are not lovable or worthy. For example, if you do something that makes you feel dumb, or bad, or incompetent, or unloved, *you* bear the guilt and depression. You will beat yourself up and anguish and blame yourself.

These feelings are not helpful to you. If you do not understand that you should forgive yourself, then you will continue to live with your fears, not with love.

So, forgive yourself for attacking, being depressed, or hating. It's alright; you are human. Do not blame yourself and feel guilty that you are bad or evil or stupid; you are not. Forgive yourself and feel peace. Let go of the idea that you are to blame, or your guilt and anger and fear will overwhelm you. The Universe forgives you; do not fight the Universe.

The greatest lesson in forgiveness is so misunderstood. They said he said, whatever is loosed in heaven is loosed on earth, and whatever is bound in heaven is bound on earth. This means simply that, if you let it go, it is gone. If you do not *let it go*, it is bound to you.

It does *not* mean that some man in a black robe decides whether or not god forgives you. God and the Universe have already forgiven you. The key is *you* forgiving. If you forgive, the burden of fear is removed and love replaces it. If you do not forgive, *you* bear the weight and burden of fear yourself and you keep it in your heart and your soul.

If nations do not forgive each other, they remain separated from peace; they remain at war. Nations think it is weak to forgive and strong to attack. How is that conducive to a peaceful world? All these principles apply to nations, which are simply groups of individuals.

Let's look at a few examples of forgiveness and how it works.

Traffic

Fairly simplistic, but effective. You're driving down the highway. You are a good driver. Suddenly, a guy in a red Porsche speeds by you, pulls into your lane, and stops in front of you to turn left without using a blinker. You are enraged, because this rude imbecile could have killed you in an accident, or at a minimum forced you to slam on your brakes and come to a screeching halt or veer sharply around him. You feared for your safety, and that is understandable. Your emotional response was first fear, then anger. You indicate your anger, and then go on down the road.

You might retain that anger by telling all your friends and co-workers, reliving the scene dozens of time in your mind, calling the guy a jackass and worse, and questioning his legitimacy. If you had the opportunity, maybe you would have shot and killed him. It ruins your entire day. You are in a bad mood and nothing else happens right for you all day long.

It is guaranteed that this guy is not worried or bothered. You could kill yourself, and it wouldn't really matter to him. He doesn't care that you're angry. Maybe he thought you were going too slow and didn't let him into the lane, or something like that. Maybe he was rushing to the hospital because his wife just went into labor, so he was not thinking clearly. So, who carries the burden of this fear based emotion, anger? You do.

As an alternative, you could forgive him; just let the whole thing go. You may discern for future reference that men in speedy sports cars should be watched carefully, or that you should be more sensitive to others around you, or perhaps it even reinforces your dedication to driving more cautiously and using your blinker to signal your intentions (always a good idea in life; communication). Then your day would not be ruined by your failure to forgive. It takes some practice to recognize your emotions, to witness and understand your emotions, and then let them go and forgive, but it is an authentically powerful thing to do. And it mainly benefits you and brings peace to you and to the world.

Fat

That's you; bordering on obese. You've always been fat and now you're fatter. You may not mind being fat and may be happy. But, if you're not, being fat can make you unhappy. Of course, you can blame it on many other factors so that you don't have to feel it's your own fault. If you had to take responsibility for your actions, then you would be the one responsible for being fat, and that means you might not be a good person, right? You desperately fear not being a good person and being lovable.

You can blame your parents; they fed you. You can blame them also because you didn't have enough money, so you had to eat lots of carbohydrates and fast food. That's all there was, there were absolutely no other choices, right? And besides, it's a genetic thing; it has nothing to do with you, it's genes. You also can blame the school; recess was boring, and there was no good athletic equipment, and all of the other kids were fat, too.

Now, you can also blame your job. You have to work long hours and take the bus home and then deal with the kids. You don't have time to exercise or the discipline to eat a moderate amount of food. You're a victim of so many other external factors, and of course, you do get depressed, sometimes because you can't do things other people do, and you'll probably get diabetes and have your feet amputated and then die.

Enough, already. You made choices every day. *You can* make the choice to overcome what some might call disadvantages (I call them challenges and opportunities). And get this; *no one else can make these choices for you.* If you blame someone or something else, you are only doing so because you are afraid to make the choice yourself.

Today is a new day. The first thing to do is not to blame someone else. Do *not* be a victim; it is a self-fulfilling prophecy. Forgive your parents, and the school, and the fast food. Most importantly, forgive yourself, you didn't know what you were doing. Now you do. Forgive the past. Let it go, but start out today - after you forgive yourself - and learn what you need to do to get healthy so you can enjoy life. Go to the library and get books to read about nutrition and exercise. Is that so hard? Stop going to fast food restaurants. Begin walking each day. Get some dumbbells and use them. Forgive yourself, every moment. It's not your fault; it's not anyone's fault. It just is, or was.

Abandoned

Your father left your family. He moved in with a woman who is not your mother. Now he wants you to call her "mom." He says your own mother is a bitch. You hate him.

Your father has his own reasons for making the choices he made. He is responsible for his choices in a civil sense, because the legal system imposes requirements on him (and your mother, too). The Universe does not, however, obligate him. He believed he would be better off, perhaps learn more about life and love (or perhaps about anger) by separating from your mother and seeking a new path or choosing a new partner in life.

None of that ultimately affects how you will lead your life. We have many situations and relationships in our lives, some fun, others not. The way we choose to incorporate them into our life is our own decision; only our own.

You are angry with him because he left; *you* feel abandoned. But he did not leave you; he only made a change in his life that he felt was *right*, that his soul dictated to him, one way or another, for better or worse. You're afraid that you will be alone, that you will never have a happy life, that you won't be loved, that you can't have the loving family home that all your friends have, and that other people will think you're somehow responsible or bad or that he didn't love you enough and that it was your fault. So, you withhold expressing your love to him. You want to punish him, because he has deprived you of the opportunity to be happy .

Not. No one can deprive you of the opportunity to have peace of mind, the ultimate and most enduring happiness. Some situations make it very difficult to be happy, no question; but that's where it is so very important to forgive. You will never be alone, you cannot be abandoned, no one ever leaves you in truth, because they are the same as you, connected to and with you, because you are peace and love and perfection and the Universe *never* leaves you.

Depression

How can I ever be happy? Every day is such a burden. I am not worthy to have love. I can't do anything right. Nobody really loves me, at least the way I want to be loved. I am too tall and have ugly wrists. There is no hope for a happy future. I will never have a warm house with lots of friends. I worry that everything will go wrong. I am so sad.

Dear one, *there is nothing to fear.* You are love, and love springs from you whenever you let it. The glass is not half empty, it is half full. The moon is not dark, it is full *all the time.* Your individual circumstances are the result of your own choices. The Universe teaches us through our lives and our choices. There is no one else from whom to learn the lessons of love, except ourselves. Even if someone tells you this, you must believe it and know it yourself.

There are so many things in life that are not immediately enjoyable. Most people do not like getting up at the crack of dawn and going to work, or doing laundry, or weeding the lawn, or doing homework, or talking with the boss. But these are not evil or bad things; they are just part of living. And part of your life. Therefore, they are precious, and should be precious to you.

Once you recognize that your depression is based on the fact that you have fears, you can address them and then forgive yourself for them. It may be hard to do. You must be able to inquire deeply into your feelings to find out what it is that you're really afraid of. My guess; you're afraid of not being loved or having love. Know that we *all* have fears, but that you can overcome them and have peace of mind, love, and be happy and satisfied. The Universe will provide exactly what you need when you need it. So, let go of your fears and have peace.

Murder

The bastard raped my daughter and killed her. He took away from me the most special person in my life. She was so tender, so young. And he is so *evil*. I hope he is put to death, for that is all he deserves. I hate him with every fiber of my being, and will always hate him.

Of course, this is a tragic situation. I hope I never have to face the death of one of my children, much less in a brutal fashion. But it can happen. Nothing can bring your daughter back. You need to grieve the loss. Grief is a form of fear based emotion, because we so fear the loss of our loved ones; their death is the closest reminder of our own mortality. As with many emotions, there is strong love mixed in. We have such love of the person that the combination with the loss can be devastating.

So, experience the grief. Remember your daughter; as you are able, look at her pictures, the videos of her playing, touch the things she made for you, sing songs for her, write stories about her, cry. Witness this strong emotion. Use it to teach you about life. But don't let it drag you down.

Isn't it obvious that the man who killed your daughter is ignorant? Ignorant of the true meaning of life and love. A man who does these things is so afraid of his own shortcomings that he seeks absolute control and power over others. It is a losing and failed effort. He cannot find love that way, but he doesn't know it. He may have to be punished under the civil laws of our society, but if you attempt to punish him too with your hate, you punish yourself by injecting *his* hate into your own heart. You will not be able to have peace as long as you hate; if you think you can, then you are simply mistaken. Forgive, and let it go. It's hard, but let it go.

Abuse

The nice, friendly parish priest betrayed your trust and sexually abused you as a child. He made you perform oral sex on him, and he did the same to you. He even raped you. You feel dirty and shamed and angry. You hid the scar for so long and now the wound is uncovered. Others release their anger, and so you do, too.

These victims of abuse band together and feel one another's pain and lash out. They say "their lives were ruined" by these despicable acts. That may be right for some of them, but only because it is a self-fulfilling prophesy.

It is fine and socially appropriate to seek justice through the civil system. No one will say that what happened to them was fair (although there truly is no fairness or unfairness in the Universe). No one will defend the priests or the church. But is it helpful to continue to allow the perpetrator of such abuse to have control over them? Is it useful for them to feel unlovable, or unworthy, or guilty their entire lives? Should they go to their graves feeling that some man ruined their lives by having sex with them? How can they avoid this?

Forgiveness, that's how. They shouldn't let those priests ruin their lives, and isn't today the first day of the rest of their lives? They may have deep emotional scars, and many people do, but the way to eliminate the fear and anger and guilt is by letting those deviant acts go and forgive the priests. They should get on with their lives. It may take time, and many may not be ready to forgive, or want to forgive (wallowing in pain and agony is very attractive to people, generally speaking). But peace follows from forgiveness; teach those priests the lessons that they thought they were to have taught you.

Shyness

Being shy is clearly based on fear. You are afraid to speak up and say what's on your mind. You have a fear that people will not like you or think you are stupid. Then, they will not want to be friends with you, or they may not respect you; another indication that you are afraid you are not lovable or will not be loved.

This shyness may also be born out of a deep respect for other people and for harmony in the world in which you live. That is love based behavior, but fear mixes in when you are afraid that you will cause others to be upset or that you will disrupt *their* peace. Admirable, but you need to be fulfilled in yourself and protect yourself and learn to live the best you can. And those other folks are truly responsible for their own peace, not you. So, don't worry about that.

Do not fear that sticking up for yourself is a bad thing. You have to do it in order to find your own peace and love. Don't be afraid to find your passion and do it; don't let your fear keep you from your peace. You have to forgive yourself for being shy, and simply must do what you need to do. Let go your fear of what others think. They may think you are stupid, and heaven knows we are not all geniuses, but so what? They may be more ignorant of the way to peace than you.

Cheating

You know your girlfriend has been cheating on you. Since you travel and only see each other a few days a week, and she is from here and you're not, she gets around. You know she has been out with other men, and she doesn't always wake up at her own place. You know it because friends tell you and because you simply know it (souls do *know* these things).

So, what are you going to do? Shoot her and lay her six feet under? Become enraged and tell her if she ever looks at a man again you will beat her with a pipe? Fill yourself with anger and hate for the other men she sees, and take them out, flatten their tires, and smash their windows? Torture her children, or her mother?

Come on, get real. She is her own self, her own person. She can decide to see or sleep with other guys. You do not own her. You can try to control her, but that is only an attempt to salve your fear of being rejected and not being loved or having what you want. If you strike out and try to injure someone else because of your anger and your fears, you will end up hurting yourself more, because you will give in to fear and fail to find love. Sure, you need to decide what you want. Do you want to see her, on her terms, or not? You can tell her you don't want to have a relationship with her if she sees other men. If she does, then she is not a right fit for you. Forgive her and give her up. You don't need her for your happiness. Let it go and let her go.

Control

Your mother answers questions people ask you before you can. She tells you what to wear and what to say and what to do. She wants to make the important decisions in your life and, most of all, she wants to control you because she fears your becoming independent and then what would she do?

You love your mother. So, love her and forgive her. Just know that you will always love your mother. Talk with her, learn from her, and teach her what you have learned, too. Your relationship with your mother is one of the most important relationships you can ever have; we learn the most from our close relationships. You learn so much being the recipient of unconditional love.

But don't let her control you. Sure, when you are a minor, there are certain things you must do. Accept that, but you know you will grow up, and do not let your mother (or father, or anyone else, even your wife or husband) control you. Forgive the efforts to control, let them go and accept them, and then do what you need to do with love and peace in your heart.

Commitment

She's the right one for you, you just know it. She is the only woman in the world for you and you won't be happy without her. But she won't say yes; she's not ready.

Excuse me. You can't be happy without her, just like you can't be happy without that new sports car, cashmere sweater, or stereo system. You know those things can't really make you happy, and so it is with other people. You can have an ultimately satisfying and long term relationship with a person you love; it is worth going for if that's what you want. But don't think that alone will make you happy.

And if someone else is not ready for you, then don't be angry. You may feel anger or frustration or that you'll never find someone else. If you have peace of mind, none of that matters.

So forgive her, she just has to do what she has to do. Forgive yourself, too, and don't give in to the emotional carnage you can bring on yourself by not forgiving. If the relationship is not what you want, move on. If you are enjoying this person, enjoy her. Know that if you can both continue to forgive one another, you can live together for as long as you want in peace and love. At the same time, always do other things that will help *you* be happy and know life and yourself more; learn, do, forgive, live.

Persecution

They believe in a different god than you. Their god is the right god for them, and your's is the right god for you. But they think your god is the wrong god. You all hate one another and shoot and kill one another. You want the same piece of land. You're afraid that they'll get the land, and that your god is not the right god and theirs is, and that your culture will die out and theirs will succeed. You continue to hate them.

This could go one for generations, or till the end of time on the earth as we know it. Wouldn't that be productive? Just think, because your parents and grandparents hated them and killed them, your children can hate them and kill them, too. And the whole time you can live in great fear and not have peace. It is *your* choice, so you can do that if you want, and condemn your children to the same path.

Why? Why in the world would you make a choice in which you cannot live in peace and your children live in fear. It's obvious; it is because you are *afraid* to forgive. If you forgave them, then wouldn't that mean you were wrong and they were right? Of course not, and what difference could that possibly make anyway?

The longer you do not forgive, the more fear you will have and the weaker you will be. When you forgive, you become stronger and can have peace. What is the real meaning of one piece of land or another? What difference does it make whose god or religion is the right one? Do not fear; forgive; and give the gift of peace to your children.

Judgment

They are different than you. What they believe is morally corrupt and unethical. They dress in a manner that demonstrates their low personal values. They do not have stable family structures. Their behavior scares you.

You are afraid of them and what they do and believe, so you judge them and put them down. You do not realize that your judgment of them does not bring peace to your society. Of course, many civil actions are not conducive to a positive social order, but where to draw the line?

As close to love and peace as possible and as far from fear as you can. Freedom of speech and conscience and association allow the creative aspects of society to come out; they also allow many other thoughts and ideas to come out, but how can that hurt? These freedoms, which many of us take for granted, are based on forgiveness. We may be afraid of others, but we overcome that fear and allow them to say what they want, generally speaking, and do and think what they want; we forgive them these things and the society is more open and creative and ultimately peaceful than a society based on fear and lack of forgiveness.

They also say he said, that he who is without sin should cast the first stone. This only means, don't judge. Why is that so hard for folks to understand and incorporate into their lives?

Complaining

Nothing is ever right. There is always some problem that is someone else's fault. Nothing is ever good enough. The service is poor, the food is bad, the salad is wilted and the meat is tough, the employees are not dedicated enough, the media is opinionated, the politicians are crooks, the athletes are rich and spoiled, men are ogres and women are pathetic. Doesn't this get tiresome? Why has it become so fashionable and acceptable to whine and complain all the time? And to blame everyone and everything else?

We do need to try to have the best in our lives and to do the best we can. We want the best for our children, of course. We should discern what is excellent and what is shoddy. That's fine. But complaining all the time is based on the fear that *nothing* can ever be right for us. It is a self-fulfilling prophecy that has its focus on fear, not love. If we complain about everything all the time, how do we see the peace and love in everything?

All of these things are simply examples of how forgiveness is the key to peace. You can deny them if you want, but think about them, if you will, and see how it all works. In everything you do, think of what fears are really at play, and how forgiveness can give you peace, even though it is often difficult and seems even a weak thing to do. Understand that forgiveness is strong, and go ahead.

It is true that eventually all anger and fear and hate and injustice, and every problem there ever was or will be, will be forgiven. Everything passes. Even things you were mad about yesterday are gone, much less things you were angry about as a child. Everything is ultimately forgiven and released. Why be a hold-out to your own destiny?

Some people have learned well how to let their fears go; they give them to some deity. That solves one problem, but not all. They know how to let go, but often they somehow don't understand true forgiveness of others, or they forget not to judge others who may believe in a different deity. Any group of people in a religion who believe their deity is the only one or better than someone else's deity judges and does not forgive. If a religion judges and does not forgive others, then it is based on fear, not love.

Of course, in every action and belief, there usually are elements of both love and fear. People strive to have love, but they don't understand fear and how to forgive. Doesn't it make sense that, the more we have love, the better our lives and society will be? And that the more we have fear and refusal to forgive, the more destructive and less peaceful we and our society will be? Why not make the simple choice for peace? It is *your* choice.

Forgive the past; forgive the future; forgive yourself. And have peace.

Chapter Five *Peace*

There you have it. And you can have it. You can have peace. It is not so difficult, complicated, simplistic, or obtuse as you might believe. Just recognize the love and then the fear, and forgive everything based on fear, including your own actions or emotions based on fear. Then, you will be able to have peace of mind.

This is not a panacea for all of mankind's troubles. Life happens constantly. You will always need to wash, put on clothes, go here or there, talk and interact with people, go to work. All of these things don't go exactly as you'd like. That's not the point.

It doesn't matter if they happen as you would like, or not; they always happen. Until you die, life happens. You will have many interactions with people, animals, food, trees, weather, and the Universe. This is just life.

Study life and your thoughts and feelings and figure out as well as possible what you want and make choices that bring you to what you want. Keep making those choices, everyday, every minute. Make the choice to forgive always.

Change what you can, and expect change, constantly. Accept yourself and the life you chose. In other words, *forgive life* for not always being exactly how you would prefer it. Just know that you do create the life you have.

I believe everyone is doing their best, as best as they understand and know. But so many people do not understand how fear controls them; they think their acts are helpful and productive, though many times they are not supporting of love, but rather destructive of love.

Do not fear the future. You have nothing before you but the future. All you really have now is *this instant* in the present. Forgive the past and your fear of the future. Then, have peace in your mind and in your heart.

We discussed the love based actions and emotions. Focus on those, and the more you do, the more you will have love. As a song that flows through us, a song that we know, peace can grow. Since we are all connected at the level of the essential energy, if some of us begin to really know and understand peace, and to reject fear, peace can grow in our world like a wildfire, and flood our collective consciousness.

We also talked about fear based things. You may not be able to expel them entirely from your life; we all have emotions and feelings that confront us and guide us. Simply recognize that certain actions and emotions are based on fear. If you don't understand how a certain act or feeling comes from fear, just keep thinking about it, ask "why," and you will find that it does.

For example, if you are angry with someone at work, ask why, why am I angry? The answer may be something like: because he is a mean but successful person and you're *afraid* he'll take your job. Whenever a reason for an action is that you're "afraid" of something, then that is a fear. When you realize this, you will also understand that these fear things are weak and take you away from love and peace, and from your home with the life energy of the Universe.

Look deeply at your fears. Don't be afraid of them. Consider them, witness them, study them. Don't dwell on them; don't wallow in them; don't surrender to them. When you find out where your fears come from, when you know what you are afraid of, accept them, and eliminate your fears through forgiveness. If you are not ready yet to forgive others or yourself, that is your decision; but do so as soon as possible, because you are the one who bears the fear in the meantime, until you come to know peace.

You know that you clearly see and feel the peace at times; at your daughter's graduation, sitting at home on a Saturday evening with a nice drink in front of a fire with your loved one, and when someone smiles at you. Decide that is what you want.

Decide right now and every minute that what you really want is peace and that you will have it. Let those discernible moments of peace and love and bliss become etched in your consciousness. Learn to also see hate and anger and depression and hopelessness for what they are; the fear of being human and not having love. It's not always easy to recognize your fears and to forgive, but it works.

We learn about love and fear and forgiveness through every relationship we have in our life. Our loved ones and family play enormous roles. Don't fight with them, try to understand them. Recognize that our relationships reach to every living and nonliving thing we come in contact with. Every person we talk or work with, or groups of people, teach us about life.

We learn also from our relationships with dogs and cats and cows and horses and birds and mice and fleas and mosquitoes and flies. We learn from our dealings with plants, too; the rose that smells so sweet, the grass in our yard, the weeds in the sidewalk, the tall pine trees crusted with snow, the oak trees tall in the forest. You only need to think about your relationship with them to know them and learn from them.

No one else can learn for you. You must learn these things for yourself. You are responsible - the only one responsible - for how you feel, and for your choices. No one else can make you feel sad, or happy, or stupid, or great, or short, or fat, or learned, or experienced, or worthy, or unworthy. All of the other things in our lives, in our Universe, lead us to the places where we feel these things, but each and every one of us is the only one who can feel or learn for each of us. And only you can pick love or fear.

Be the best, smartest, fittest, most tuned in person you can be, so that you can maximize the life you have.

Don't get in a rut. Take walks, go places, read, do different things, embrace chance, don't give up and fizzle out. Be healthy, and enjoy how much life can bring you, even as it gives you what you may not want. You need everything that you get.

We all recognize that people believe lots of seemingly crazy things. One religion's teachings seem bizarre to another. Some believe in god, some in the devil, and some in the power of money, the artificial and meaningless system of exchange we have developed to get along in our society. Some believe in eating bugs, others cows, others not. Some also believe in strength and power and control and war and torture and fear and death. I say, why not believe in peace and love?

We know how much man can accomplish to get what he wants. Man can practically bend the physical world to achieve his goals. When man was cold, he learned how to make fire and she learned how to make clothes. Now we have heat for when we're cold, and even air conditioning when we are too hot. We can control the air and climate in large buildings, theatres, airplanes, submarines, buses, cars.

Humans wanted to go faster, so they learned how to ride horses, then invented wheels and rode in wagons and now automobiles that drive us everywhere, no problem. We wanted to cross rivers and oceans, so created boats and ships. We wanted to fly like the birds, and learned how to do it ourselves in planes and helicopters and jets. We wanted to go to the moon, so we went.

We wanted to remember how things looked, so we learned how to take photographs, and then moving pictures. We can recreate football plays and school plays, exactly as if we were there, and look at them years later. Television allows us to see what is happening miles away, at the same instant, from many different angles.

We wanted to hear music again, so invented the phonograph, now CD's, which play that music again and again, whenever we want. We desired to communicate with others of us who were far away, so first we developed the telegraph, then the telephone, now cell phones, so we can practically talk with anyone on the planet at any time and let them know our thoughts.

We can now find almost any information on the internet about anything instantly. Electronic messages travel around the globe in seconds. We send the ghosts of large documents across wires, or now without wires. We are electronically linked to everyone and all the knowledge we have.

We can prolong life, with medications and operations. We can change our bodies, with exercise, healthy food, and knowledge. We can stave off pain with drugs and even create life.

We can do anything we want.

But, what is all this really, if we can't have peace? The easiest thing to do, to have peace in our world, seems like the most daunting task. The news is of bombings, and war, and murder, and snipers, and rape, and pillage. People rage at other people. Do we truly understand how insane and crazy war and attack are?

We set up our civil systems with the goal of peace. Actually, many countries and nations do well. Many people have peace in their lives, live in peace. Billions of people live in peace, although many don't really even realize it.

Peace based systems engender creativity. Governments allowing freedoms of speech and expression and thought and association and religion flow with the love and energy of the Universe and are creative and successful.

Fear based regimes, where order essentially results from the fear of death, stagnate. We all know this. But still we should forgive and love these hateful, fearful men; they know not what they do. We just need to do what's necessary for peace.

If we eliminate all of the fear based activities, by forgiveness, then we can have peace. But as long as people believe war and attack and anger are strong, and believe that there is evil, then the inherent weakness of these things will continue. Only when people understand that forgiveness is strong will we have that chance at world peace.

Of course, our civil systems can not only forgive. Our tangible and societal need for public order demands that people who are deemed to violate the laws and restrictions that the system dictates must be treated in a way that does not permit such behavior to continue. But we should focus on teaching peace and love and forgiveness, not punishment, and helping all people to learn peace and love and forgiveness, for our own sake.

The way to do this, I believe, is one person at a time. I do not have all the answers, but I believe in my heart that we all can have peace. And peace starts with each of us, to make the choice for peace and love and to recognize that fear based actions and emotions hold us back from peace.

We all can be teachers of peace; we can teach each person we come in contact with about love and peace. We can teach people the true source of their pain and the chaos and war in the world. This is the highest goal, to teach peace and to teach love. You teach others all the time; teach them peace.

You may not believe all of these things I have said. That doesn't matter; this is not a religion. But if you make one choice, make the decision to have peace. Don't wait for the other person. Go first. Don't be afraid of peace; don't be afraid to forgive. Believe in the love and peace in your heart of hearts.

Every person will have and find different loves, passions, and fears. And each person will have unique avenues or channels to peace and love. Some may meditate; others worship; or find peace through rocks. To each his own.

Some folks may have extreme physical or mental disabilities that would make it very difficult if not impossible to do these things themselves. However, I believe that any thinking human being can learn to address and overcome fears to a certain extent and achieve at least a relative peace of mind. Why wouldn't that be worth a try?

Others may believe that they are dependent on drugs or other potentially healing or therapeutic factors. Fine; whatever. Do what you must do. Drugs are necessary and can be effective in reducing pain; certainly outside forces affect our bodies. But I believe that ultimately the power of the energy of the mind is supreme over the physical body.

Believe in your - and our - worthiness and perfection. Don't believe in evil and badness, but just see such human defined actions as based on fear. Then understand how others come to do what they do. Forgive the fear, and their fear.

Try to understand the reasons you feel the way you do and why you do the things you do. Think about whether all this fear and love stuff makes sense to you, that's all I ask.

I just know that I would rather lead my life believing in peace and love than in anything else. I believe peace and love are practical, not war and anger and hate and attack. I don't know why we shouldn't believe - truly believe - in a world of peace.

I don't think people understand fear, or the role of forgiveness in eliminating fear. This book is meant to help people know peace, so that they may enjoy their own lives, their own perfection in the Universe, rather than waste it in squalor and hate and war and death. It seems like such a simple choice. Choose love and peace over fear.

Pax Vobiscum.

Salaam Aleikum.

Shalom.

Peace and love be with you all.

Biography of Author

Jefferson Glassie has been studying and writing about concepts of peace for some thirty years. In *Peace and Forgiveness*, his first book published by Peace Evolutions, LLC, he provides a simple guide for finding peace of mind through forgiveness. His main goals in life are to learn and teach peace.

In addition to writing, Jeff is an attorney in Washington, DC representing nonprofit organizations. He has written and spoken extensively on nonprofit legal issues. He also established his law firm's Well-Being program.

Jeff lives in Maryland with his life partner Julie Littell, and he loves his children all the time. He also plays acoustic blues harmonica as much as he can.

Excerpts from:

Poems of Peace and Forgiveness

Jefferson Glassie

From Above

When you look
down
from above,
don't you
see
love?

From a plane
in the sky,
as far as the eye
can see,
there's love.

Life

is us
you and me.

Bees and fleas
cats and dogs
rocks and logs
rivers and seas.

The same
energy
is us
you and me.

If

you judge
you condemn
yourself

because
you are

the same

as the one
you judge.

Is this it?

Who could
ever imagine
snowstorms
gentle rain
baby's breath
rose thorns
sperm whales
mountain tops
child's play
sun sets
moon rises
palm trees
lion roars
bird songs
desert winds?

Why not know?
Heaven is everywhere.

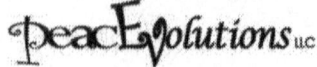

Order Form

Fax orders to (301) 263-9280 with completed order form.

Email orders by logging on to www.peace-evolutions.com

Telephone orders by calling (301) 263-9282.

Postal orders may be sent to: Peace Evolutions, LLC
P.O. Box 458-11
Glen Echo, MD 20812-0458

Please send the following:

☐   Peace and Forgiveness, book $14.95 each   quantity: _____

☐   Peace and Forgiveness, audio CD $14.95 each   quantity: _____

☐   Poems of Peace and Forgiveness, book $12.95   quantity: _____

We will honor all requests for full refund on returned items.

Please send more free information on:

☐   presentations

☐   other publications and information

Name: _____

Address_____

City: _____ State: ___ Zip: _____

Telephone: _____

Email address_____

Sales tax: Please add 5.00% for products shipped to Maryland addresses.

Shipping and handling:

United States: $5.00 for first book/CD and $2.00 for each additional item.

International: $7.00 for first book and $5.00 for each additional item.

Payment:

☐ Check   ☐ Credit Card

☐ Visa   ☐ Master Card   ☐ Discover   ☐ American Express

Card number: _____

Name on Card: _____

Expiration date: _____

www.ingramcontent.com/pod-product-compliance
Lightning Source LLC
Chambersburg PA
CBHW031256290426
44109CB00012B/611